W.A.R.

Watch | Assess | React

The Ultimate Guide to

Personal POWER

and Safety

Tonya Dawn Recla

PersonalPOWERexperts.com

Third Edition - April 2015

First Printing, 2007

Published by:
Tonya Dawn Recla
Glendale, AZ 85308

PersonalPOWERexperts.com

Printed in the United States of America

Editing and Formatting by:
102nd Place LLC
Scottsdale, AZ 85266

*To my husband who encourages me
in the discovery of my personal power
and gives of his own so generously.*

Table of Contents

Foreword

Eight years ago I wrote the first edition of *W.A.R.* The April 16, 2007 shooting at Virginia Tech sparked my desire to share what I knew about fear and safety. My undergraduate and graduate study gave me the cognitive tools to understand the power of individual thought processes, group-think, and socialization. My training as a soldier and counter-intelligence agent taught me the physical techniques to control my personal space. I recognized that people needed some easy-to-use tools to help them combat a pervasive fear mentality that started long before 2007.

I remember, as everyone does, feeling the world fall from beneath my feet on September 11, 2001. Even today, typing that date from eleven years ago makes it feel like yesterday. I know I'm not alone. I don't have a tragic story to share about that day, but I felt it. I felt it again in 2002 during the Washington DC sniper spree. I faced it head-on during Basic Training as my drill sergeants taught me how to kill people in various ways. And I felt it again in 2007, even as a government agent, when I heard about the shootings at Virginia Tech.

But then I wrote *W.A.R.* I wrote it from a passionate place of powerful desire to help the nation deal with the fear. I wrote it from a place of my own fears and battles. Unbeknownst to me, I wrote it as a way to catalyze my own change. As I processed through the information in the book, I found the connection I so desperately sought. As is the case with most creative projects, this stemmed from a place so deep inside of me I had no idea the depth, the magnitude or the multitude of correlations it had to other aspects of my being.

I initially thought I'd close the book following the chapter on mass attacks. But that felt empty and devoid of the underlying purpose behind the entire project. As I opened myself up to addressing the fears inside of me, I realized the magnitude that a pervasive fear mentality has on a society. It goes well beyond fear of personal safety. It strikes the cord inside each of us that is intricately and primitively connected to all others. The cord that reminds us we are part of something bigger than ourselves and the stranger sitting next to us in the restaurant, library or movie theater, matters.

Since 2007 my journey took me through entrepreneurship, marriage and motherhood. The dismantling of my fears and inner struggles regarding my own personal power that began when I wrote *W.A.R.* further intensified as I opened my world to my husband and his children. Then my identity dove headfirst into complete transformation the day my daughter opened her eyes to me. My seeking and questing for self-awareness took on a whole new level of purpose when I asked myself who I want to be for her.

The concept of personal power is no less powerful to me now, but it is much more personal. The information from the first edition still remains valid today, but my perspective on it has shifted.

I updated the POWER chapter with a more comprehensive picture of how I approach this topic and added a more recent question I've answered regarding children in the Q & A section.

I also added an additional article at the end of the book: *Conflict Resolution or Heart-Centered Communication*. I struggled with leaving in the article about the incident at the University of Maryland. I certainly wrote that from a place of passion and, I daresay, a bit of fiery "I am woman, hear me roar" mentality. Ultimately I chose to include it in this edition because I don't think the conversation about female personal safety has progressed much since then. But I offer a different type of article as a means of balancing the conversation a bit.

I have so much more I want to include regarding the topic of personal power, but I didn't want to sacrifice the emphasis on personal safety this particular book offers. Of course, that just opens the door to many more POWER books down the road. Stay tuned...

Tonya Dawn Recla
Phoenix, Arizona
April 2015

Introduction

*Named must your fear be
before banish it you can.*
Yoda

Fear

What's the single factor that guides most people's lives? Fear. Most people plan their lives, careers, years, and days around some form of fear.

Face it, fear is the single most effective motivating factor in our society. Advertisers use it every moment of every day to encourage you to buy products you don't need: fear of getting/looking old, fear of not being attractive, fear of being fat, fear of being unloved, fear of not being able to have sex on demand, fear of being the last one on your block to have the newest gadget, car, haircut, etc.

Your parents used fear to keep you in-line. Everyone remembers the sing-song chant of "you'll shoot your eye out" in *The Christmas Story*. Advertisers and parents use fear because it works.

It works because people don't like feeling that they're powerless in a world of chaos. People want to feel like they have control over their lives and their circumstances. This is the entire reason why terrorism is so successful.

Terrorism's biggest crime isn't the actual incident of terror, it's the fear it implants in people because of its seemingly random nature. It's the threat of violence that governs most people when it comes to terrorism and violent attacks. Terrorism controls the lives of more people through mental captivity than it does through its actual acts of violence.

How many people changed their lives, their patterns, and their behavior immediately following the terrorist attacks on September 11, 2001? The entire nation shut down temporarily. The fall-out afterward affected far more people than were in the towers that day.

The violent attacks at Virginia Tech in 2007 caused the same type of impact. At colleges and universities all over the nation, students, faculty, administration and parents asked themselves where the next attack would occur. The feeling is it could happen any-where at any time.

And it's true, the threat and the concerns are real, but the fear doesn't have to be

So, what can you do about it? What can you do to free yourself from the fear of random and violent attacks? What can you do to build confidence in your ability to assess the potential danger in a situation before it becomes perilous?

What can you do to take back your personal space? Plenty. You're not powerless.

You may not know when or where someone will choose to use violence against you. But you can learn a few simple steps that empower you to decipher the seemingly random and mysterious behavior of others.

By removing the mystery, you greatly increase your chance of being able to respond to a potential situation before it turns violent.

How different would your life be if you could walk around with your head held high, in a constant state of awareness, knowing you have the ability to handle any situation you encounter? Savor that thought for a moment.

Does it sound like the issue is being over-simplified? Maybe it is. Or maybe you're used to hearing issues of personal safety discussed in overly dramatized and seemingly random ways.

W.A.R. – Watch, Assess, React

It's natural to view tragedies and violence through lenses of fear. And make no mistake; there's a random element to violent attacks. No one can give you advice on or train you to prevail in every dangerous situation.

However, you can increase your odds greatly by employing techniques that will make you less susceptible to targeting and more likely to walk (or run) away from a situation unharmed.

As you continue to read, realize that some of the tips and techniques discussed are simple and should be considered common sense. Before you dismiss them, however, ask yourself how frequently you employ them in your life.

Think about the aspiring professional athlete who knows she'll run faster if she would practice running, but chooses instead to sit on the couch and then wonders why she isn't winning races. Or the college student who knows he should study before an exam, but opts to play video games instead.

Get the picture? The point is, many people know some of the techniques discussed, but they choose not to use them. Most people have been trained in some form of personal safety, even if it was only their parents telling them to look both ways before crossing the street. But, most people were trained using a fear-based methodology.

What good is it to tell people if they don't do something they might die? Automatically the brain switches to the counterargument of, "I may die anyway." That method is as productive as telling a college student if she doesn't go to class she won't get a good job -- not real persuasive at eight o'clock in the morning after a night of partying.

The point is you might not die if you don't use these strategies. But, by using these strategies, you might survive a situation you wouldn't have otherwise.

Or you might find yourself beginning to walk taller and stand more confidently knowing you're aware of your surroundings and ready to respond if necessary. You might find yourself venturing out somewhere you wouldn't before because you were scared. You might find yourself looking people in the eye and saying hello because you know that confident friendliness is a turn-off to potential predators.

You might, accidentally, spread a little joy in the world, simply by educating yourself about personal safety. Bet you never heard joy and personal safety in the same sentence before.

Whatever motivates you to utilize these techniques, lock it in and continue reading. You'll find information you already know presented in a new way and new information presented for the first time. But all of it will aid you in transforming your life to clear the murky, senseless concept of safety and plant solid, powerful tips and techniques in your psyche that'll benefit your life in ways you can't begin to imagine.

This method of personal safety has so many hidden benefits. It's like taking a birth control pill that also makes you lose 10 pounds. By developing confidence in your ability to handle potentially violent situations, you learn to use the same techniques in dealing with others. You engage your inner strength and act in positive ways.

Heck, some people think confidence is dead sexy. And who doesn't want to be a little sexier? The point is don't read this and go through the motions because you're afraid of dying. Read this and go through the motions because you love living.

The rest of this book is purposefully broken into chapters based on developmental steps. Some people like to read through the book in its entirety first to get a feel for the work they'll be doing. Then they go back and reread the individual developmental steps and work through the W.A.R. Tips. Personally I recommend reading the first three chapters and mastering the POWER concepts before moving on.

I also suggest keeping a journal of your observations, thoughts, and feelings as you practice the tips provided. This will allow you to track progress on your path to personal power and safety. In addition it provides a reference if you feel yourself start to backslide.

There's no timeline for going through this growth process, it's individual and specific to each reader. Each developmental step builds on the previous one and only you know when you're ready to take that next step.

My Path to Personal POWER and Safety

*We have stories to tell, stories that provide
wisdom about the journey of life.
What more have we to give one another than
our 'truth' about our human adventure
as honestly and as openly as we know how.*
Rabbi Saul Rubin

With most paths the twists and turns rarely show themselves along the way. Only in

retrospect does the journey from Point A to Point B make any sense. My path to personal power and my arrival in the arena of personal safety proved no different.

When I sat down to write this book, I asked myself, Why me? Why did I feel a compelling urge to enlighten the world about power and safety?

The answer both amused and surprised me. Through a series of seemingly unrelated events in my life, I arrived at a place where my innate desire to develop into something more and my overwhelming need to exist in a secure world merged.

This amused me because I never saw it coming. Never, ever, could I have predicted my arrival at this point in my life even if someone had given me the map.

It surprised me because throughout my life I always prided myself on my ability to analyze critically, even the events of my own life. Again, it took me arriving at a particular location in order to put the pieces together.

As I dissected, reviewed and pondered my life at particular stages, I began to see the pattern. For some reason each time my path led me to a proverbial fork in the road I chose to take the path of *most* resistance.

Literally. My resistance, my family's resistance, society's resistance, you name it, the resistance linked arms and wrapped themselves around the entrance to fork option number two chanting, "Hell no, we won't go!"

Power Barriers

But despite the years of socialization and influence urging me to take the easier path, I consistently fought through what I termed *Power Barriers* in order to experience something different. These barriers became my right-of-passage transition points from one identity to another.

In my lifetime I've held identities and titles like, Daughter, Sister, Student, Writer, *La Guera* (Blonde Girl), Teacher, Trainer, Global Marketing Specialist, Graduate Student, Caregiver, Soldier, Special Agent, Entrepreneur, Master Instructor, Wife and Mother. But none of these, individually or collectively, can illustrate the significance of the transitions between identities.

These transitions acted like the sand that brushes against ocean stones polishing them through the years. Each Power Barrier molded, squeezed, pulled and yanked me through experiences that challenged my worldview and forced me to define – for myself – the concept of personal power.

Personal POWER vs. Personal Safety

Ultimately this led me to explore and comprehend the concept of personal safety at a level no one ever talked about.

Through all of my years of education and Army and government training, no one ever suggested that our perception of safety is inextricably tied to our ability to maintain our own personal power. Never. The conversation always stopped at concepts like self-defense and understanding the enemy.

But that's only half of the conversation. If you approach personal safety without exploring your own Power Barriers and your own beliefs about personal limitations, you've already determined the outcome of any situation you encounter. You already know the extent to which you'll go to defend yourself because you've told yourself it's impossible to go further.

Simply by not addressing innately held beliefs, you sentence yourself to repeating behaviors...regardless of how dangerous the situation may become.

In the Beginning...

As I traced my development back through the events of my life, I realized my propensity for analysis started early. Even as a young girl I questioned everything. I realize this is not unusual for most children. Curiosity and childhood may as well be synonyms.

But I took it further. I wanted to know the who, what, where, when and why of everything. (My counterintelligence inter-viewing instructors would have been so proud!)

My mother once told me I asked questions as a child most adults never dream to ask. I explored and dissected the world around me to the extent that I became obsessed with understanding.

As the years progressed, I started to think my insatiable desire to know was a detriment. It led me to gifted education and honors-type study programs, but I fully embodied the concept of "analysis paralysis." My questing and searching identified the multitude of options this world holds and the information overwhelmed me.

I grew up hearing messages like I could do anything I set my mind to and the world was my oyster. Believe me, I realize what a gift these messages were. And I later discovered that not all children hear these words. But the sheer magnitude of possibilities truly made my thirst for knowledge unquenchable.

This didn't become obvious until I arrived at stages in my life when "normal people" made decisions about their life path. When "normal people" chose a direction and started walking. And not only did they start walking, but they kept walking on the same path in order to achieve the originally chosen goal.

This process and Tonya's concept of the world did not mesh. I stumbled even with the first part of that process: the choosing. Something deep inside me felt like choosing one option naturally meant I sacrificed all others.

Because of this I never had a favorite color, song, movie, ice cream flavor, animal, cartoon character, nothing. I mean, how does one look Speedy Gonzales in the eyes and explain he just didn't measure up to the Tasmanian Devil?

But even when I did make a choice, I often tired of it quickly. When I was fourteen I applied to work at Burger King. I excitedly donned my BK apparel and joined the workforce.

It took one week before I learned everything available to learn and decided I had no interest in pursuing a management track. Some people happily worked there for decades, content to do the best BK job possible. I marveled at that level of dedication. But I didn't understand it.

Power Barrier #1: Family Ties that Bind

I have gathered a posy of other men's flowers;
only the string that binds them is mine own.
Montaigne

As I entered the "real world" after high school, my pattern of indecision continued. I always knew I'd go to college. I attended the only publically funded college preparation school in the nation...college wasn't optional. But beyond that I had no idea where I wanted to attend.

Much to the dismay of my guidance counselor, I pursued enrollment in the Honors College at Arizona State University (ASU) for the simple fact that my "hometown" and "acceptable" choice for an instate school, University of Arizona, only offered an honors program, not a college.

No amount of explaining smoothed things over with my guidance counselor so I gave up trying. It wasn't the first time I rocked the boat and certainly wouldn't be the last.

I loved college, but had trouble choosing a major. Even as everyone around me seemed completely secure in their chosen career field, I struggled deciding on a major. I didn't like the idea that I was trying to answer the age-old question, what did I want to be when I grew up?

Again, in retrospect, I realize choosing a major is as important as choosing what kind of car to drive. You have to live with it for a while, but you'll forget about it a few years down the road.

One day my roommate, who knew exactly what she wanted to do when she grew up, brought home Gordon Allport's, *The Nature of Prejudice.* I picked it up and got hooked. These were ideas I never thought before and concepts no one ever taught me.

I asked her why she had it and she explained it was assigned reading for her intercultural communication class. I changed my schedule and enrolled in the same class.

That began my love affair with issues of culture and communication techniques. The further I delved into this subject the further I wanted to go.

I was fascinated. I still didn't totally understand what people meant when they talked about culture. I mean, I understood about other cultures, but I never really thought about my own...until I attended a leadership retreat.

The focus of the retreat was culture: race, ethnicity, gender, sexual orientation, religion, etc. Basically it explored all varieties of social identities.

Before leaving for the retreat I received a list of required items. On the list was: bring something that identifies your culture.

Huh?

Well, let's see...I was born in Kansas, but we moved to Arizona when I was two. So Dorothy and Toto were out. My Euro-mutt ancestry included German and French, but all I could say in German was, "When monkeys fly out of my butt" (random, I know, you can thank Mike Myers). And no *parlez-vous français* so that was no help.

I can best describe my childhood cuisine as eclectic and I'm pretty sure we took all traditions and rituals from a hodge-podge of other cultures.

So, I did what any over-actively minded person might do, I brought words. I went to the retreat with a piece of paper carrying the quote by Montaigne at the beginning of this section.

As creative as this might have been, I quickly discovered that the point of the retreat was to rip me apart at my assumptive seams, fling my white-washed mindsets far and wide and begin the process of rebuilding me with the very preliminary hues of awareness.

And I cried.

The entire three days of the retreat, I cried. Even as I reached hungrily for more, even as I heard the words others shared about their worldview and, most significantly, their perception of me, I cried.

I stood with as much resolve as I could muster and stared my life in the face. I looked through the eyes of people who grew up in very different places, with very different influences, carrying their own very different perceptions of the world...my world.

This would become my first Power Barrier. As my world crumbled apart and lay scattered at my feet, I took a good hard look. My introduction to awareness left me battered and bruised, but happy. For the first time I realized the power behind my insatiable curiosity.

Without that extreme desire to know, I wouldn't have persisted through such a painful experience. And I never would've listened when others explained in agonizing detail the way they experience the world.

That pivotal moment, combined with so many others that followed because of it (to include a summer spent living in Tijuana, Mexico), allowed me the opportunity to decide for myself the degree to which I wanted my cultural, familial, ancestral, and tribal roots to determine how I experienced the world.

Power Barrier #2: Sugar and Spice...

My studies and subsequent life progression led me to explore all of my various social identities, to include gender. But not with the same in-your-face type force mentioned above.

I always struggled with the concept of being a girl. I was quite content to be a girl, but I didn't want to be girly. I made that distinction at a young age when I associated girlishness with an inability to control emotions and a desire to engage in relationships rather than experiences.

I think this had something to do with my grandfather always telling me, "There'll be plenty of time for boys after school." His intent, of course, was that I finish school before losing my head in a relationship.

But when does one "finish school?" I'm not sure Grandpa thought about the fact that I could, theoretically, continue school through the duration of my life.

I did, in fact, return to ASU after a brief stint as a Global Marketing Specialist for a Fortune 500 company. The company suffered a setback and terminated 300 of us in an effort to reorganize. I gladly took my severance package and ran back to ASU and a shiny, new graduate program.

So, once again, I was a student and that meant, per Grandpa's instructions, boys had no place in my life.

Of course I'm over simplifying things. I dated and had relationships. Well, brief, very brief relationships. But the desire in me to understand myself and the world around me ran counterproductive to long-term relationships.

Even my friendships tended to be brief with very few exceptions. One of these exceptions, a girlfriend I met in the fifth grade, once told me that I recognize when something is over faster than anyone she's ever met. And I have the conviction to walk away.

It probably says something significant about me that I took that as a compliment.

The other aspect of this girl-against-the-world mentality is I enjoyed feeling free to do what I wanted to do when I wanted to do it.

I'm the type of person who randomly decides to enlist in the Army after attaining a graduate degree because she watched 9/11 happen on TV. And, quite frankly, I didn't want a boyfriend or husband always around trying to figure what leg of Tonya's Wild Ride he was destined for next...or worse, trying to stop me.

But ironically, despite all of my thumbing my nose at convention and doing things my way, I still struggled with the gender issue.

As my life progressed through the Army (by the way, people told me I'd never make it through Basic Training...I did) and into federal service as a counterintelligence Special Agent, I faced head-on the concept of gender.

In addition to running espionage investigations, I operated as a member of a counterespionage surveillance team. Throughout my stint on the team, I saw members come and go, but always the number of men greatly outweighed the number of women.

At one point in time, I was the only woman on the team. And surveillance is a grueling occupation at times. The long hours and stressful work make the camaraderie of team that much more important. I didn't feel any camaraderie with this team.

The team dynamics did not mesh with my own. I always felt a bit like I was swimming upstream. I knew men, I understood men, I like men, but something just didn't click. I felt like I was always arguing or debating or competing.

So I decided to get help. I figured the one person in our office who could understand what I was going through was a female Army Colonel. Any woman who climbed the Army ranks to O6 surely understood how it felt to be the only woman around.

I sat down to talk with her. She listened intently and nodded empathetically. Then, in true Army fashion, she said, "Leave."

Leave?

"Yes, leave," she said, "go do something else." I can do that? I can just walk away? That concept completely contradicted my entire Army training.

She continued, "Do you know how lucky you are to have figured out what you don't want? Some people go their whole lives and never know. Look at it this way. You could continue doing what you're doing, but it's like putting a round peg in a square hole. You can do it, but it doesn't feel very good."

And that was it. That was the sage advice from a woman who knows what it's like to operate in a man's world.

So I officially resigned from chasing spies and went back to investigating them.

Now this was the known and readily acknowledged aspect of gender I battled. It wasn't even much of a battle since I voluntarily enlisted in the Army and continued as a government agent, both areas of extreme man-ness.

But as with most significant growth phases in life, there was a deeper, darker battle raging beneath the surface. Only after years of self-analysis and heart-dissection do I realize the impact of two separate but intimately entwined events in my life.

I hesitate to write about these because I now choose to view them through spiritual lenses. My favorite saying is, "There are no victims in the spiritual realm." I don't even know who said it, but I use it to remind me that if we choose to look for deeper meanings, the initial, superficial label of victimization falls away and the lesson to be learned rises to the surface.

I hesitate because the topic of sexual assault is highly volatile (if you don't believe me read *From the Hen House to the Lion Den* at the end of this book) and even more highly debated.

But the powerful growth and understanding I achieved because of these experiences and my willingness to explore them on multiple levels far outweighs any potential hurt feelings or misunderstandings.

When I was 16 years old I was assaulted. I didn't call it that, in fact, I thought it sucked and was inconvenient, but I didn't label it. Others labeled it for me. When the word "rape" was used it felt alienating and inaccurate.

Despite my obvious victim status, a piece of me knew the experience served to teach me something. I saw therapists, read books and talked to a number of people regarding moving on from such a personal attack.

But nothing helped. I wasn't devastated by it, I was confounded by it. Again, something inside of me knew I could learn something huge from it, I just didn't know how to find it.

I searched with varying degrees of intensity for eleven years to find some kind of explanation, some justification for the experience. And instead of finding clarity, I enlisted in the Army.

Somewhere in the midst of nine weeks of Basic Training I realized exchanging military training for self-actualization wasn't a bad trade-off. As I donned the identity of soldier, I stopped looking for victim definition and practiced target shooting instead.

Here's the funny thing about spiritual lessons. If you choose to ignore them, they tend to come back. Now I don't know fate's plan or why the cosmos turned left instead of right, but I do know because I chose to ignore the nagging feeling I had that the lesson ran deeper, I was presented with another opportunity to explore it.

After years of combat training, advanced weapons training, aggressive driving training and additional personal development, it happened again.

During a surveillance mission with the previously mentioned predominantly male surveillance team, I was sexually attacked.

The grueling hours and stress led to drinking and poor decision-making.

Again, I don't mean to be flippant about the incident. But the similarities between the two situations ran deep. Both times the reason I did not fight back was because I had more concern for other people involved than I did for myself. Both times I thought longer and harder about the fallout from making a scene and demanding justice than I did about the impact on my soul.

It wasn't until I had to accept the fact that sixteen years after the first incident, armed with an arsenal of self-defense techniques and weapons, I allowed the same thing to penetrate my sense of self.

Why?

Revelation

I was willing to publicly defy stereotypical roles and argue with anyone who thought I couldn't do something because of gender, race or any other social characteristic.

I developed atypical relationship patterns and challenged anyone who deemed them immoral or superficial. But I bought into the idea that I was powerless in ways so subversive I didn't even know I needed to break free.

Despite the graduate degree and combat training and jumping off of towers and top secret clearance and expert weapons qualifications and intense driving ability, **I was afraid.**

I didn't realize how afraid until I started rereading the book, *Beauty Bites Beast: Awakening the Warrior in Women and Girls* by Ellen Snortland. I'd purchased the book years before when I first pursued enlisting, but had never read it cover to cover.

This time was different. This time when I got to the section on "Saying No" my perspective on my life changed completely.

Have you ever found yourself in a situation where you know you've been building up to a certain point and then you hear something or you watch something or you read something that somehow shifts everything into position?

That's what it felt like when I read this section of the book. It was only a few pages, but it was the glue that adhered all the pieces that previously drifted about separately.

We've heard our entire lives that no means no and we're allowed to say it. But how many of us believe that? How many of us really believe we have the right to say no and fight for our own preservation, our own desires?

I've spent the last sixteen years of my life wondering why, if I'm such an intelligent, strong, independent female (and I always have been, even as a young girl), I couldn't find it within me to fight when I was sexually attacked. Or how I would repeat the behavior years later after I had combat training, expert handgun skills, and even though I "knew better."

I've never been a shy person and it really made no sense to me. All of my friends from childhood to adulthood will say that I was always the strong one, the outspoken one, the one most likely to come to someone's defense. I almost got in a bar fight with three men one time because they were inconsiderate to one of my girlfriends.

I didn't go looking for fights, but I certainly didn't back down from them if my friends or family were involved. Why then was I unable to use that same ferocity to come to my own defense? And why during the second time, even when I'd had years to assess the first situation and finally had the physical skills to fight back (I was a trained Army soldier for crying out loud), did I still freeze?

It made no sense – until I finally understood the relationship between respecting your feelings and protecting the part of you that feels. I could express my opinion, but I didn't honor how I felt.

Later in life I would joke that white, middle-class Americans don't talk about their feelings, they just tell you what they think. But truthfully, I had no idea there was a connection between my self-preservation and my ability to defend myself in a violent situation.

I didn't know that I started a pattern a long time ago of not speaking up for myself or protecting my inner essence. I didn't know it affected my ability to react strongly in a dangerous situation.

And I certainly didn't understand the fight, flight, or freeze defense mechanisms available to us and how each impacts our lives. But by piecing these experiences and information together, it all became clear.

My story isn't unique. I know many women who can claim similar situations. But it's not just women who fall into this trap. There are men who are so far removed from where they started they've forgotten what it's like to speak up.

I know men who are miserable in their jobs, in their marriages, and in their lives, but they continue day-in and day-out drudging along life's thankless path because they think it's what they're supposed to do. Some of them have been away from their feelings for so long, they don't even realize they have them.

And for what? So at the end of the day you can say you did what was expected of you or you handled it like a man? Do you think there's some sort of award for that? When you're miserable you make everyone around you miserable also. There's no consolation prize for that – you just get to live a wretched life.

In a weird way, I was lucky to have a rape in my past. As least I had somewhere to start. But in all my retrospection, I had to acknowledge the events themselves were nothing more than a culmination of years I spent denying me.

How many people do you know have no idea who they are or at what point they gave up on themselves? How many people wander around this world thinking they're "fine" and life's meant to be lived without color, without passion (true, gut-wrenching, heart-exploding passion, not lust)?

And then we throw in fear of terrorism or being attacked randomly and the powerlessness that entails. Is it any wonder we're a world full of cynicism and listlessness?

All of these thoughts struck me at the same time. And I realized I'd been clinging to this Power Barrier for dear life. The final barrier was the one that had been dwarfing me for so many years, I didn't know what it felt like to breathe freely, unencumbered by the suffocating effect of others expectations and unspoken disapproval should I step outside my bounds.

It wasn't saying no to big things like people who said I couldn't join the Army or chase spies that I struggled with, it was saying no to the everyday minutiae that slowly, over time, build you into the person you truly are.

It was saying no to friends who had expectations of me or family who wanted me to live my life in a particular way or men who wanted more than I wanted to give them or strangers who wanted to be in my space. And I acquiesced for fear of hurting their feelings or worse, upsetting them to the point of violence.

It was saying no to the daily demands and requests that weren't in my best interest or just weren't what I wanted to do. It was saying no to my male co-workers because they thought their way was always the right way. It was saying no to my hairdresser because she thought she knew what I wanted better than I did. It was saying no to the server who continued not to bring me what I ordered regardless of how politely I asked.

It was saying no to a litany of stupid jokes, dumb asides, and ingratiating flirtations, assuming the people involved had no idea how idiotic they sounded.

Instead, I made excuses for people and accepted silently these demands and requests because it made other people happy or made other people's lives easier or made other people like me with no regard for the impact it had on my soul, on my spirit, or on my ability to live fully.

Well, no more. The clouds have lifted, the ties have been severed and the Power Barrier destroyed. This awareness of being trapped for years without knowing it created within me the passion to live every moment to make up for the time I gave up blindly.

More importantly, this awareness was the missing link between the life I was developing and the life I need to live now. The link between who I allowed myself to be and who I want to be now – for me, for my husband, for my daughter, for the world.

I mentioned that the path I took only became clear in retrospect. Without each of those pieces placed precisely where they were, I wouldn't have had the foundation to reach this level of knowing.

As I exposed the first Power Barrier, the next one became evident. The first battle prepared the way for the next.

No one is better positioned to share these lessons regarding being vigilant than I am. With my education, experience, and self-awareness, I offer a unique perspective that has the propensity to change people's lives and alter our social consciousness about personal power.

I paved the path and the directions are simple. Place your feet where mine have been. Your path will be unique for you, but by following the steps I lay out, your success is inevitable...our success is inevitable.

Being vigilant is a state of awareness assisted by cognitive and physical tools that create empowered and confident individuals who have the ability to take back their personal space and themselves. And these individuals en masse have the ability to take back our schools, our cities, and our nation.

POWER

The most common way people give up their power is by thinking they don't have any.
Alice Walker

POWERinity

I don't know anyone who would say they don't want to feel powerful. I know some people associate power with corruption, but that's not power's fault.

Those people tend to disassociate themselves from power because of the negative connotation they assign it. But when conversations revolve around personal strength and conviction, I've never met anyone who claims they'd rather feel weak and insecure.

And it seems that women are very comfortable talking about *empowerment* but the moment conversation turns to *power* something changes.

Why?

What is it about the concept of power that makes women uncomfortable?

The answer lies in the highly complex connotation of power and the even more complex socialization of women. The concept of power corruption is only one piece of this complexity. The bigger issue is how women perceive themselves as powerful beings or power*less* beings.

So what does it mean to be powerful? Does it mean to be strong? I looked up strong in the thesaurus and was taken aback when I read two synonyms for strong are masculine and manly.

I guess that says it all. As a society we associate power and strength with positive characteristics for men and, while not necessarily negative characteristics for women, atypical. This isn't a new conversation. Sixteen years ago I debated the genderfication of language for one of my classes.

I'm not lamenting that things haven't changed. Things have. Today I can watch *Domino, Enough, Aeon Flux, V for Vendetta,* and *The Brave One* to see women kicking ass.

What I am suggesting is that in order to have an honest discussion about power and our views on it, we need to address gender assumptions.

So, instead of writing an epic on how language shapes our reality and how our reality is closely tied to gender specific nuances in our language, I propose we move away from this stilted place.

I'm not comfortable suggesting men need to be more masculine or women need to be less feminine. Or that both sexes need to get in touch with their masculinity. Let's do something different. Let's let men be men and women be women and revel in our separate "inities."

When we talk about developing our personal power, let's acknowledge we all have inner strengths that look and talk and act differently. I propose we develop our individual *POWERinity*, apart from and inclusive of our genders.

Right now you're saying, "Ok, Tonya, so what in the world is *POWERinity*? How do I get it? Do I want it?"

POWERinity is the heart of who you are when you're not concerned with embarrassing yourself, looking cool, saying the right thing, doing what you're "supposed to," or being someone you're not.

POWERinity is the piece of you screaming to get out, silenced only by your fears and perceptions of your role in the world. And how do you get it? You have it. All you have to do is step aside and let it be what it's meant to be.

Do you want it? I think each of us secretly craves a connection with the most internal and powerful piece of ourselves. Some of us have lived so far away from the center we don't realize it's there. Of course, this is a personal question and can only be answered when you allow your inner presence to reintroduce itself to you. I'm pretty sure you're gonna want it.

Now maybe you're asking, "Is this just a semantic-laden marketing ploy to get us to use a word you made up to say the same thing others have been saying for years?" Maybe, but that's not to say it doesn't have merit.

Think about it this way. If we continue to equate power and strength with masculinity and manliness what does that do for our women and girls? Moreover, what does it do for our men and boys?

If you raise half of the population to believe power and strength aren't inherent to them and you raise the other half to believe they have full claim to it, what does that do to our perceptions of each other. It sets an impossibly high standard for men to achieve and a dangerously low standard for women to reduce themselves to. And we've been doing that for years. I'm thinking it hasn't been working out very well.

So, humor me, let's try something new. We have nothing to lose. Women are getting raped, people are getting murdered, and relationships are wrought with confusion between identity-stunted people. Really, what do we have to lose?

The POWER of No

As I mentioned above, I was shocked when I finally grasped the power of saying no. We hear it all the time, but it seems that the full impact of this tiny little word has been lost on some of us.

By simply going through the motions of saying no, with conviction, you send a message to your brain and your body that the situation you're in isn't conducive to your well-being and it sets wheels in motion to counter it.

Essentially, saying no gives your body and brain permission to fight back. Just the act of saying the word centers your mind and calls upon your resolve.

The will to say no in a dangerous situation starts with saying no to any situation that doesn't promote your greatness. Every day we're faced with decisions about what to do, what to say, and how to act. And every day we have the choice to make decisions that progress our development or thwart it.

When we choose to limit our growth by conforming to someone else's will or someone else's version of what's right for us, we tell ourselves we don't matter and we're somehow "less than" someone else. Some people buy into the concept that complete sacrifice for the good of others is saintly.

Without getting into a debate about religion and God's will, from a completely secular perspective, how helpful can you be to someone else if you aren't addressing your own basic needs?

Maslow's pyramid of needs tells us that security of body and health is second only to our need for food, water, and excretion. Love with friends and family, esteem, and self-actualization are dependent on a solidly built foundation, including the safety of self.

You can't benefit others without first benefitting yourself. We've all heard the old adage of you can't give away what you don't have, right? Consider this before you agree to do something for someone else before you address your own needs.

Women especially seem to have trouble with this concept. For some reason, certain women consider themselves the burden bearers and can't seem to say no even at the risk of personal detriment.

Another argument I've heard is that putting your needs before another's makes you selfish. It's hard to believe, but the effect is actually the opposite.

By addressing your needs and developing a strong sense of self you have the ability to affect your world in wonderful and positive ways.

People who are whole, complete in their mind, body, and spirit, have the inner strength to offer the world everything they have to give and their supplies continually replenish themselves.

People who ignore their needs have very little to offer and have no foundation to rebuild themselves when they've spent all they have.

Ah, but what about the children? Now, don't get me wrong, I don't have children but I understand that parenting is a complex and complicated process, regardless of gender. But no matter how you feel about your children, sacrificing everything for them does nothing to help them.

If you're not healthy and whole, any example you set for them is laden with inherent messages of weakness and loss of self. The ideal situation is to be whole and resolved in your self-preservation before you have children, but if not, realize that any move you can make in this direction ultimately serves your children better in the long run.

Surely we want more for our younger generation than to offer it models of helplessness and emptiness.

My point in all of this is if you don't develop patterns of standing up for yourself and creating within you strength of preservation, you won't have anything to call on in a dangerous situation.

If you buy into the idea that people have the right to walk all over you in your daily life, chances are you'll carry that with you into a perilous predicament.

Start practicing by saying no to the seemingly little things. The first thing you'll notice is those things really aren't that little. Built up over time, the demands on your time, your patience, and your sense of self, create a persona you adopt as your own.

As you start to refuse their existence in your life, you realize it feels good to speak your mind. It feels good to defend your right to live the way you want to live and do the things you want to do.

So, if learning to say no has so many positive benefits, why don't more people do it? In addition to being socialized not to say no, many people are afraid.

The list of fears is endless, but it includes fear of reprisal, fear of rejection, fear of violence and fear of disappointing others.

If your buddy calls and wants you to go watch football with him, but you'd rather stay home and read a book, do you go just because he wants to?

If your girlfriend wants to have sex and you really just want to go to sleep, do you have sex because if you say no she'll pout or use it against you later?

If your boss asks you to stay late even though she agreed to your strict schedule when she hired you, do you agree because you think you can't afford to lose your job?

When a guy you're talking to at a bar walks you to your car and tries to kiss you, do you let him even though you're not attracted to him? What if it's an empty parking lot, do you worry about the risk of angering him and the situation turning violent? Sometimes it's just easier to comply, right?

Sure it is. I'm not claiming these situations are black and white or life isn't full of healthy compromises. I'm just suggesting that days, months, and years of agreeing just to agree build a pattern in your body on a cellular level and allow you to rationalize away your importance in favor of everyone else.

Despite your fears, once you start asserting yourself into your life, you'll realize the benefits far outweigh any perceived repercussions.

Additionally, you'll start to realize you just don't care what people think or if they don't understand. The ones who do will respect you and your decisions.

People will start to comment on how you look different, more confident, and how your behavior inspires them to do the same.

Marianne Williamson wrote, "And as we let our own light shine, we unconsciously give other people permission to do the same. As we are liberated from our own fear, our presence automatically liberates others."

And there it is.

The next time you think you're doing someone a favor by limiting your own greatness, by acquiescing to something, anything, that isn't in your best interest, remember this quote.

You're adding nothing good to the world by denying your greater self and you're sucking the energy from the rest of us. So stop it.

W.A.R. Tips

- Practice saying no to small things. Before agreeing to any social event, ask yourself if you really want to do it. If not, don't do it.

- Use words that strengthen you. Pay attention to gender specific words and their latent meanings. Start using *POWERinity* to define who and what you are.

- At the end of every day, ask yourself if you lived your full greatness that day. If not, identify situations when you dimmed your light and make a vow not to do that tomorrow. Be nice to yourself in this process. You're breaking habits you took years to develop. Be kind, but resolved.

Be Vigilant

*The aim of life is to live, and to live means
to be aware, joyously, drunkenly, serenely,
divinely aware.*
Henry Miller

Live in the Pink!

The first step in gaining control over your environment is to start being vigilant. Vigilant is defined as "being alertly watchful, especially to avoid danger."

Anyone who's been involved with law enforcement knows to be constantly aware of her/his surroundings. The purpose of being vigilant is to train your eyes, mind, and body to remain in a state of awareness that allows you to react to situations more quickly that you could from an unaware state.

Truthfully, you should strive to be vigilant at all times. When you get home for the night and are locked away safely from the world, you can let your guard completely down, but until then, it's best to remain vigilant.

Now before you start arguing with me about having to be vigilant at all times, let me help you understand what this means. I like to call it "Live in the Pink!"

When I worked as a government agent, my job required a high level of competent driving ability. So I went through aggressive driving training, where they taught us how to drive safely at over 100 mph in traffic. The only way you can do this is if you're aware of everything in front of you, around you, and behind you.

The trainers taught us using a color continuum to understand this concept. The continuum went from white to red. The white zone is a state of complete unawareness. Using the driving metaphor, this would be the person talking on a cell phone, eating a burger, painting nails, and driving a standard transmission simultaneously.

Okay, that's extreme, it's also the person fiddling with the radio or replaying the fight they just had with one of their friends over and over again in their head. The white zone encompasses any person who is distracted at all from the task at hand. This is the person who doesn't see the school bus stopped three cars ahead or the emergency vehicle two cars behind in their rearview mirror.

The color red is used to signify the opposite end of the spectrum which is total heightened awareness. The red zone is where people enter as they have to respond to a crisis.

The pink zone is used to signify the place in between (they used orange or yellow; I like pink, that's what happens when you work and train in an all-male environment...no pink...face it, guys, any four year-old can tell you when you mix white and red you get – pink!).

For our purpose, pink signifies a manageable awareness of your surroundings. This continuum signifies the importance of maintaining vigilance. If you're driving around in the white zone and a cat runs in front of your car, the time it takes you to get to red, where you can react, is too long to avoid killing the cat or swerving into another car you didn't know was there.

However, if you drive around in the pink zone, you have time to react to surprises with precision because you're already aware of everything around you. You know where you can swerve to avoid killing the cat and hitting another car.

So if white is bad and pink is good, isn't red better? No. The reason you don't want to stay in the red zone all the time is the same reason training people using the fear mentality isn't effective.

First off, you can't maintain that level of heightened awareness at all times. You'll go crazy.

Secondly, it's not practical. There's no point to living life if you're going to walk around convinced that you'll have to respond to a crisis at any moment.

Think of it like dieting. Let's say you love ice cream. How long will you stick with a diet that requires you to stop eating ice cream for-ever – and ever – until you die? But, you know you can't lose the weight you want if you eat ice cream every minute of every day.

In the long run, the more logical approach is to adopt a sensible diet and eat ice cream as an occasional treat, right? There's a way to love living your life and be aware at the same time.

Live in the Pink!

W.A.R. Tips

- For the next few days, do whatever it takes to remind yourself to Live in the Pink! Write post-it notes and put them in your car and your office. Remind your family and friends. Set an alert on your watch, phone, or electronic calendar to periodically nudge yourself to be aware. Keep doing this until it becomes second nature.

- For a solid week don't listen to the radio, talk on your cell phone, or play audio books while you drive. If you typically drive with other people in your car, make a total silence policy for the next week. If your mind starts to wander about the day's activities or the last fight you had with your friend, bring it back to the present moment. How does it feel to be totally aware as you drive?

W.A.R. – Watch

We cannot create observers by saying, "observe",
but by giving them the power and the means for this
observation and these means are procured through
education of the senses.
Maria Montessori

In order to master being vigilant, you first need to understand the "Watch" step in the W.A.R. acronym.

In the beginning this might feel unnatural, but you truly have to start watching everything around you all the time. The reason for this is that most people live their lives in the white zone. They have no idea what's going on around them.

Observation

I observe people all the time and am still amazed when I see people walking around with their heads down or distracted by their phones, their iPods, or their daydreams.

Again, I don't think you have to convince yourself that you could be in danger any second of any day, but wouldn't it be nice if you had time to prepare if something did happen? You buy yourself precious seconds by simply lifting your head, looking around, and taking note of your surroundings.

For the next few days, I want you to start noticing the people you pass and the cars you see. I want you to be able to notice when things seem different in an area you enter daily or when you see the same car every day.

This doesn't automatically mean that the situation is dangerous, but if you observe your surroundings daily, you develop a baseline of normalcy. If you don't have any idea what most people look like as they walk around normally because you've never bothered to watch, how are you going to know if someone is acting peculiarly?

In the next few days, try to make note of everything you see. If you live in a particularly crowded area this is going to be more difficult than for the folks living in rural areas, but that's your environment so you need to get used to it. Just do your best and keep at it.

The reason I suggested doing this for the next few days is that you'll notice it starts to get easier. Eventually you'll notice things without realizing it. You'll find yourself able to recall details you wouldn't have even seen before.

Going back to the car metaphor, where do you look when you drive a car? You scan, right? What would happen if you just stared at the road five feet in front of you the entire time and didn't look at the speedometer or your mirrors? Exactly. So, why would you treat walking in a grocery store parking lot any differently?

Start making a habit of scanning your surroundings everywhere. Keep your head up, raise your eyes, make eye contact, say hello, heck – smile. There's nothing more daunting to potential attackers than for you to embody a confident, empowered stance and to smile in their faces as you walk by.

When you maintain this posture, you're saying to the world that you own your personal space and you're aware of what others are doing with theirs. You'd be amazed at what you'll see and the potentially harmful situations you'll be able to avoid – hopefully without ever knowing it.

Practice

The key to mastery is practice. Practice being vigilant. Make a game out of it – count how many blond haired people you see in a day, count how many Volkswagens drive by (anyone remember Punch Bug?), play name-that-make-and-model with your kids or friends, just start observing your surroundings.

Pay special attention to the areas around your house, your job, your school, your kids' school and any areas you frequent. Watch how people interact when you're sitting in a restaurant.

Without being obvious try to remember what people are wearing, their general descriptions, and their body language. If you're dining with someone else who wants to develop their skills you can quiz each other on how many people are in the restaurant, how many women, how many men, how many windows, how many doors, and anything you can think of.

The point is to retrain your brain to see and retain details. Continue this practice until it becomes second nature. As you continue to build your observation skills you'll notice that you don't have to work as hard to absorb as much.

You'll also start to notice a change in the way you interact with your environment. Just by observing your surroundings you change the way you present and carry yourself. This will add to the self-esteem we began building earlier.

As a side note, one of the interesting by-products of being aware of your surroundings and walking confidently is you decrease the desire to be hyper-vigilant.

The relationship is as self-esteem builds, panic and nervousness dissipate. This, in turn, reduces any feelings of helplessness that cause you to look around nervously and react suddenly to innocuous situations.

Basically you become Joe (or Josie) Cool because you know you have the knowledge and tools you need to react appropriately to situations. And who doesn't like a little confidence?

W.A.R. Tips

- As you start being more aware of your surroundings, keep a journal. Write down the make, model, color, and license plate numbers of all the cars you can recall. The first few days it might just be one or two, but as you progress you should be able to remember more.

- In your journal, write down the people you remember throughout the day. Don't include your friends, family, or people you know. Try to remember people you saw and details about them. As you write down information about them, try to visualize them in vivid detail. This isn't that difficult, we do it all the time with people we're attracted to. Just use that same ability to recall people you notice throughout your day.

- Use your journal to record the development of your confidence as your levels of awareness grow. It'll be fun to look back on this journey and see how far you've come.

W.A.R. – Assess

The only real valuable thing is intuition.
Albert Einstein

By mastering step one, Watch, you now have a baseline understanding of your surroundings. But, as I'm sure you've already guessed, that's not enough.

Once you've established an understanding of everyday behavior, you have to begin to assess the information you receive.

There are two ways to assess information and you need to master both. The first way is mental assessment.

Mental Assessment

As you gather information about your environment, your mind automatically wants to make sense of it. By going through the motions of observation you already started implementing mental assessment.

Now I want you to start directing this assessment. Let's take the restaurant example. When you're sitting in a restaurant observing

73

your surroundings, you should make note of the number of doors and windows and where they're located.

As you do this, your mind starts to make determinations based on the information. If you notice there's only one visible door in the restaurant, your mind should move quickly to question if there are doors you can't see.

You also should be trying to determine the quickest path to the door if leaving rapidly becomes necessary. Now let me reiterate. You shouldn't be afraid to go out to dinner for fear you might have to escape quickly if someone attacks the place.

I'm going through these steps to make sure you start directing your brain in the ways you want it to process information. Once it gets used to these steps, you'll do them without thinking and the information will be stored for use if necessary. But it won't provoke feelings of fear unnecessarily once you get in the habit of thinking this way.

Another thing you should start to notice is where you can sit in a restaurant, coffee shop, or bookstore and have the best visibility.

When paying attention to your surroundings starts to become important to you, you'll find yourself requesting certain tables and choosing certain seats because they allow you to watch the door or observe others unobtrusively.

Please don't use these techniques to ogle unwitting people. By all means, check out people if you want, but don't be creepy. Nothing good comes from that.

Let's move on to observing your neighborhood. Let's say you've been practicing observation for two days and both days you recognize every car that passes your house.

Now, on day three a car drives by you don't recognize. Again, you don't jump to conclusions and assume the person in the car is there to cause harm.

The reason for going through these steps each time is for practice, not because you just crowned yourself the town crier. Instead, you train your brain to make note of the vehicle make, model, and color. Try to read the license plate and look at the occupants of the car, if possible.

By going through these motions, you start storing information in a different way and can make recall easier if need be.

Lastly, let's talk about how to assess information you gather when observing people. One of the best things you can offer as a witness to any crime is untainted, unbiased data.

It's difficult for witnesses to recall details that aren't infused with their own biases, filters, and memory confusion, unless they're trained to do it. You can develop these skills by looking at people in a different way. When you look at people, make note of their height (using a range of two or three inches), weight (using a range of one to ten pounds), race/ethnicity/culture (to the best of your ability), hair color, skin tone, build (stocky, thin, medium, etc.), clothing, shoes, facial hair (presence of, color, style), and any distinguishing characteristics (visible tattoos, scars, abnormal gait, etc.).

If you find this type of profiling difficult, practice first with your friends, family, and acquaintances. Ask them if they mind answering your questions regarding their height, weight, and race/ethnicity/culture. Then test yourself. It isn't a perfect science, but it definitely gets easier with practice.

Another reason to make note of this level of detail is you can know with certainty if you've seen someone somewhere before. Do you ever get that feeling that you've seen someone before, but you can't recall where or you don't know for certain?

As you start to make note of details, you'll be able to recall the person more quickly and have a better chance of remembering where you first saw her/him. As you can imagine, this is a helpful skill in possible stalking situations.

But what you might not think about is the usefulness for networking and rapport building, as well. Again, there are many hidden benefits to becoming aware of your environment and honing skills to better assess information. Just go through the motions and you'll start to see your life chance in many positive ways.

Intuitive Assessment

The second piece to the assessment step is intuitive assessment. This piece is as important as the first piece, but many of us have forgotten how to do it.

What's weird is intuitive assessment is the easiest and most natural thing in the world to do, but as we grow older we often shut ourselves off from this ability.

As children, we're so in tune with our instinct we basically make decisions based purely on gut feeling. If you watch children interact with strangers, you can't deny that kids feel people on a different level than most of us do as adults.

Kids are quick to tell you when they don't like someone or make it obvious when they're not comfortable. This is because kids haven't developed the mental boundaries that block our intuition.

For some reason as we grow older we equate instinctual reaction to immaturity. We shape ourselves so methodically that we tend to shut off our communication with that natural ability to assess people on a level deeper than our five senses. In order to truly assess a situation, you have to learn to reconnect with that instinct.

Don't fret, all is not lost. Despite your efforts to ignore your instinct, it hasn't left you. You're never truly disconnected from that innate ability.

You may choose to pretend it's not there, but much like dealing with your annoying kid brother, closing your eyes doesn't make it go away.

So let's work on opening your eyes, or specifically, your eye, the one you've been given to see without seeing.

Now, don't check out on me, this is pretty simple stuff and even if you find yourself repulsed by anything metaphysical, just bear with me. By implementing a couple simple techniques you won't be able to deny the power of reconnecting with your instinct.

And it's so easy, the only logical conclusion is it's natural and an ability we're meant to sharpen. This is another one of those areas that has hidden, magical benefits.

By reestablishing your link to your instinct, you increase your ability to interact positively with others. Who doesn't want to be able to understand people a little better? Might make dating or marriage a little easier.

So try it out, wear it around for a while, and if you don't think it enhances your ability to assess a situation, what have you lost? But I guarantee if you practice this with an open mind, you'll appreciate the lesson.

So, Tonya, let's do it. How do I reconnect with my inner think tank? First off you have to realize that you can't know by thinking.

You can derive an answer by thinking, but you can't know an answer by thinking. The significance of this semantic somersault is you have to learn to rely on something other than your mind.

Now trust me, this lesson couldn't be any harder for anyone than it was for me. I'm the queen of living in my mind and rationalizing everything into whatever nice, neat package I desire.

So the absurdity you feel trying to figure out how to know without using your mind is the exact same absurdity I felt when I first encountered this concept.

But as you start to redevelop your relationship with the place where you do know things, you'll understand what I'm talking about. But, first things first, let's find that mecca of memory, the knower of all knowledge, your inner enlightener.

In order to do this, you have to get past your mind. Now, you've been developing your mind for quite some time and, if you're anything like me, you thrive on intellectualism.

This probably has served you well in most areas of your life...not this one. Intellectualism is the devil to intuition's Eden.

Everything you've learned and think tells you your mind is the central knowledge power. Not so.

Your mind is one way you interpret information, but your intuition is another. There are many techniques to accomplish reconnecting. There's no one way that works for everyone, so you'll have to test them out.

If you don't have any experience with this, here's one way that might work. The goal is to center yourself. People who do yoga or practice meditation have probably developed their own method or adopted someone else's.

Once you begin to recognize how it feels to be centered, you don't have to go through these motions every time, you'll just be able to take yourself there. Pay attention to this concept because it's going to be necessary in the React phase.

An easy way to start centering yourself is to sit quietly in a place where you won't be disturbed. Breathe normally and just think about your breathing. Don't try to change your breathing, just pay attention to it. Close your eyes and concentrate on the center of your body. Try to think about the very center of yourself internally.

This should somewhere below your neck, above your belly button and between your shoulders. It doesn't have to be precise; the point right now is to go through the motions.

Once you allow your instinct to take over, you'll be guided there naturally. Start out doing this a few minutes each day and work up until you start to feel grounded.

You'll know when you start to feel it. The more time you spend centered the more natural it will feel and the easier it will be to listen to your intuition.

So, right now you're probably asking, "What the heck does this have to do with assessing a dangerous situation?" And, no, I'm not advocating that you stop in the middle of a perilous situation and ask the bad guy/girl to wait a minute while you center yourself.

What I am advocating is you become adept at this technique in order to better serve your ability to assess situations intuitively.

The purpose is to gather information in the watch stage and then assess the information using mental and intuitive tools. The point to using both methods of assessment is one might pick up on cues the other doesn't and vice versa. Here's an illustration:

You're walking around a track at a park. You're concentrating on your pace, but maintaining an awareness of your surroundings (because you're walking in the pink, of course).

You haven't seen anyone else at the park the entire time you've been there. It's still light out, but moving rapidly toward dusk. You turn the corner and see a guy jogging toward you.

You immediately begin your process of detailing: he's 5'11" to 6'1", 190-200 lbs., white, black hair, light skin tone, medium/athletic build, white T-shirt, black shorts, white Nike running shoes, clean shaven, and a tattoo of an eagle on his left calf (you've got really good eye sight).

As he gets closer, you notice him staring at you. Ok, no big deal, you're used to men staring at you. You maintain eye contact as you get closer.

You nod your head in acknowledgement and he smiles slightly and looks away in a publically acceptable fashion. Your mental assessment doesn't reveal anything alarming.

But because you just read a fantastic, literary masterpiece, *WAR: The Ultimate Guide to Personal Power and Safety*, you know that your assessment isn't complete until you check in with your intuition.

You've been practicing being centered and listening to your inner knowing, so you're able to switch quickly to your instinct. No warning bells go off until you're right up on him and out of nowhere your heart starts to pound.

The back of your neck starts to tingle. Your instinct is registering sky high on the creepy-o-meter. But your mind is telling you the guy hasn't done anything wrong. You have no reason to suspect him of anything, but your instinct says otherwise.

Your mental assessment and intuitive assessment conflict. This is why honing both skills is so important. There will be times when your mental assessment will tell you things your intuition can't.

For instance, your intuition won't provide you with details. It won't notice a bulge in a pocket indicating a weapon. Or a man making a slight motion with his hand, indicating to a second man some agreed upon sign for attack.

Your intuition operates on energy and concepts. Intuition will aid your mind in assigning meaning to changes in energy based on previous experience. Your mind will aid your instinct by providing details for your intuition to assess on a quantum level.

Both are necessary to develop a complete picture to inform your body how to react. So what do you do when your mental assessment and intuitive assessment conflict?

Ah, you already bought the book, so just keep reading to find out...

W.A.R. Tips

- Now that you know the steps for describing people using mental assessment, use your journal to record the people you remember using the height, weight, etc. list. See how different your list is now from the lists you wrote following the Watch step. You should now have a better understanding of what to do with information your mind collects.

- Pay attention to your development as you become more in-tuned to your instinct. You should start to feel calmer in your decision-making and less apprehensive about choosing things for your own benefit. Tuning into your instinct will make it easier for you to continue saying no.

- As you go through your day, be cognizant of whether you're using your mind or instinct to make decisions. You may be using a degree of both, but try to ascertain which mechanism you use to reach particular conclusions.

- Continue your daily centering exercises. You should start to notice the process getting easier and the minutes beginning to fly by. This will translate to you being able to center yourself more quickly, even when you're not sitting at home by yourself.

W.A.R. – React

No matter where we are,
the shadow that trots behind us
is definitely four-footed.
Clarissa Pinkola Estes

Now we get to the information everyone wants to know. Most people are shocked at the level of information they're required to endure before I tell them how to react to situations.

The reason for this, as you've hopefully already learned, is the formula for avoiding or surviving dangerous situations isn't simple.

The process becomes simple, but the deconstruction of your old habits and patterns isn't easy. I could just tell people to avoid bad situations and give them physical tools to fight back if they can't avoid them, but it wouldn't do any good.

The reason telling people to avoid bad situations isn't enough is because unless you train people to observe their surroundings and teach them to be able to assess what they see and feel in situations, they aren't equipped to determine potential danger.

And the reason just giving people physical tools and expecting them to use them isn't enough is because it doesn't take into account the level of submission most people know regarding preservation of themselves.

Fight, Flight, or Freeze

I hear it time and time again, "Why didn't she fight back? Why didn't he fight back?" The answer is simple, if men and women exhibit an inability to defend themselves daily and consistently deny the development of their greatness in their day-to-day lives, they won't defend themselves in a dangerous situation, no matter how many physical tools you give them.

Until they know, deep down on a cellular level, that they're worth fighting for, nothing you tell them is going to make a difference. The only way to begin that growth is to help them understand the myriad ways they give up pieces of themselves daily.

If you continually give up parts of your soul because you don't think you're important enough to preserve, you won't have a convincing argument to offer yourself in the face of abuse, assault, rape, or death.

This is particularly true in cases of abuse, sexual assault or rape. Because the attack may or may not be life threatening, the victim who doesn't have a clear sense of his/her own worth can easily rationalize submission by arguing survival is paramount.

Survival means nothing if you live an empty existence, one that allows you to think any abuse or assault is something to rationalize.

An assault on any piece of you is a death blow to your spirit. If you allow an assault to happen without fighting, you're setting the stage for repeat behavior in every aspect of your life.

If you're the survivor of an assault where you didn't fight back or didn't fight back to the extent you now know you can, the only way to begin the process of healing is to convince yourself you're worth fighting for, no matter the cost.

Developing through this process will help you stop the cycle of submission you began when you didn't defend yourself with everything you had.

There's no shame in acknowledging you didn't do everything you know you could do now. You did everything you knew to do at the time to survive. Now you know better.

There's a deeper, evolutionary significance to the fight, flight, or freeze issue. Peter Levine discusses it in *Waking the Tiger*. I'll try to summarize it here.

In nature there are predators and prey in every situation. Even though the same predator might be prey in a different situation, there's no confusion. For example, the fox will always be prey for the lion but will always be a predator to the chicken.

Predators, when faced with a dangerous situation are hardwired to fight. Prey, when faced with the same situations, are hardwired to flight. When prey are bested in their flight, they freeze.

Occasionally the freezing skill is used as a decoy like playing possum. If a fox doesn't have time to choose flight, it can decide to freeze as a defense mechanism.

This act of freezing in a stressful situation forces the energy that started coursing through the fox's body when it recognized danger to stop suddenly and collect.

If the fox succeeds in tricking the lion into loosening its grip, allowing the fox to run free, the fox's body automatically releases the energy as the fox enacts the flight defense.

This is why animals rarely exhibit signs of shock from trauma. They're either killed or they run away.

But the difference between the animal world and the human world is animals don't have intellectualism to thwart their natural transference of energy.

If the fox somehow were to survive the attack, let's say the lion got distracted and left the fox in its frozen state. You'd probably see the fox jump up and shake or run off anyway.

The fox knows on a primitive level that it must release the energy that was forced to a halt in the traumatic experience. If it didn't, the fox would start to show signs of post-traumatic stress disorder and it would affect the fox's existence until that energy was redistributed.

For humans, this process is further convoluted by the fact that as humans we're a little confused. Humans can be predators, prey, or peaceful cohabitants depending on the situation.

Because we don't automatically choose predator or prey status in every situation, we're not hardwired to flight or fight. This means we get to decide.

Free will is great, but in dangerous situations it can be debilitating.

When a victim of assault or trauma, sexual or otherwise, freezes in a situation and survives the abuse, without enacting either the fight or flight defense, the energy collected in the body has nowhere to go.

This is true of our war veterans and survivors of car crashes, fires, and natural disasters, too.

Without the proper assistance in the healing process, these individuals face a lifetime of random and inexplicable symptoms and diseases.

Understanding this process that Levine illustrates brings us closer to realizing that by telling people to do whatever it takes to survive an attack, even if it means submitting, is the most detrimental advice we can give.

Couple that with the fact that study after study is proving women who fight back against a sexual attack suffer less violence than women who submit by crying, begging, or pleading and the story changes completely.

Now here's the caveat, if you've been a victim of sexual assault and you froze instead of fighting or flighting (I'm just going to make that a gerund), don't be too hard on yourself.

That's what your body knew to do to survive. With the proper healing teachers, you can grow from that experience. The purpose of this book is to provide another option.

If you train your mind and body to be able to leave a situation before it becomes dangerous or to fight if you're in the middle of it, your natural reaction won't be to freeze.

You can retrain yourself with the right tools. That's why it was imperative to outline the process of connecting with your inner will to defend yourself and the importance of knowing you're worth protecting.

Get in Touch with Your Inner Child

Throughout this book I've explained the importance of reconnecting with your inner knowing, the place within you that informs your decisions on an instinctual level.

Now I'm going to tell you to get in touch with your inner child. That doesn't mean I'm going to ask you to lie on the couch and tell me about your relationship with your mother (that's a whole different book entirely).

The purpose of discussing your inner child is to help you remember there was a time when things were black and white, good and bad, fun and not fun. That was when you lived on instinct. Let's go there now.

The example I mentioned in the last chapter left you in a situation where your mental assessment and your intuitive assessment conflicted. As you passed the man jogging on the track your instinct set off alarms even though your mental assessment didn't result in anything suspicious.

Now what? How do you react to a situation that all rational thought tells you is fine, but somewhere deep within you says it's not?

You become three years old again. There's a reason your instinct is reacting the way it is. As you continue to develop your relationship with your inner self, you'll know more about why it reacts certain ways to certain things. Until then, treat your internal alarm with respect.

Any three year-old will tell you if it feels bad, it's bad. Go with that. Now, I acknowledge, it's possible that your instinct is reacting to something in your past that has nothing to do with this particular guy or situation.

So what?

Until you know for certain why you're responding a particular way, keep it simple. If part of you says the situation is dangerous, then it's dangerous. End of story.

Given this, you have mere seconds to make a decision. The very first thing you do should be instantaneous.

Even before you decide whether to stay or go, you must take control of the situation. You can't control the situation if you allow the man to run by and you continue walking with your back to him as you contemplate your next move.

If you do this and he intends you harm, you've already set yourself up at a deficit. Immediately change course. You can start walking backwards (only choose this option if you're adept at walking backwards, falling over something and twisting an ankle won't help the situation), stop where you are (pretend to tie a shoe, stretch, whatever, but keep your eyes on him), or simply turn and start following him.

The best choice depends mostly on the environment you're in. If you can get to your car quickly by continuing in your original direction, then it might be best to walk backwards or just stop and let the distance between you grow until the time it would take you to get to your car is less than the time it would take him to get back to you.

If the only way back to your car is the direction he's going, then it's probably best to follow him. Not too closely, but it won't hurt to let him know that you're aware he's there and you're watching his movements.

If he's really there for exercise, he might look at you oddly, but then it's up to him to decide if he's in danger from you.

This is key. Do NOT make decisions regarding your safety based on others' perceptions of you.

What if you follow him and he thinks you're attracted to him and you're hoping he'll ask you out and he's not attracted to you and you feel stupid because he thought, blah, blah, blah.

Or what if you follow him and he thinks you're stalking him and he starts running faster and you feel stupid because he thought, blah, blah, blah.

Who cares?

You know your true intentions and you know you were doing what you thought best to keep yourself safe. Nothing else matters.

Now after you take control for the moment you have two choices, you can remove yourself from the situation entirely or you can stay in the situation and treat it as hazardous.

The decision should be made based on your ability to defend yourself if he should attack you. The variables involved in this decision are your physical ability and skills, the presence of anything that can be used as a weapon, and the environment.

If you believe you're capable of defending yourself against this man one-on-one, or if you have a weapon (a knife, pepper spray, or anything you take when you go walking – I shouldn't have to mention this is something I highly recommend) and can determine with relative certainty that he doesn't have a weapon (you never know for sure, but if his clothes are so tight you couldn't hide a pebble in them and his socks aren't visible above his shoes, chances are good) then you might choose to continue your exercise regime.

The last variable that should affect your decision is the environment. If you're truly alone with this man and the area if fairly desolate, you may want to reconsider. But if there are people within earshot, a consistent traffic pattern, or open shops close by with steady clientele, these could work to your advantage.

Regardless of which choice you make, move your awareness from pink to red for the duration. Be ready to react without hesitation and have a plan at all times.

This is just one example of a situation that has the potential to turn dangerous. Obviously I can't go through every possible scenario and outline the decision-making process.

This process should help you with most one-on-one attacks. If you Live in the Pink! and do the watch and assess phases constantly, you'll be well-positioned to react accordingly to any situation. If your alarms start going off, following these steps:

1. Get control of the situation. This doesn't mean to control the other person, but put yourself in a position where you're not just reacting to their behavior. Make them react to your behavior if necessary.

2. Live in the red zone for the duration.

3. Have a plan to remove yourself from the situation or fight if necessary.

Relationships

There are two main types of one-on-one attacks: attacks by strangers and attacks by people you know. The attacks by people you know may be sudden or they may be abusive situations over a period of time.

The intricacies of intimate relationships and emotional ties are numerous and difficult to disentangle. I'm sure at some point I'll dedicate an entire text to the topic.

But for now I want to mention them here because I think it's important to get people to start thinking about the ways they allow abuse to continue in a relationship.

Right now I'm only discussing relationships between consenting adults or soon-to-be consenting adults (in age, not coercion). The topic of abuse in families or of children is too vast to get into here.

I will say, depending on the age of the individuals involved, the concept of saying no is a great place to start to understand how some of those situations persevere.

As I mentioned earlier, your ability to protect yourself in a dangerous situation is closely tied to your ability to protect yourself in more benign situations. Our concepts of healthy relationships have long been skewed by the media, Hollywood, family and friends, religion, and culture.

Since the inception of civilization, the rules regarding what a woman should accept or must accept in a relationship have differed from what a man can choose to accept.

This isn't breaking news. But I think we forget this when we find ourselves in relationships with others without having a strong, clear sense of self.

This is true of men and women. I don't know any men who are being beaten physically by their wives, but I know plenty who are beaten emotionally, mentally, and psychologically.

Now men, before you joke or judge, ask yourself how many times you go along just to go along so as to avoid drama or a discussion "about us." How many times do you find yourself doing things you don't want to do just because you've convinced yourself it's the right thing to do?

I'm getting away from my original point, but suffice to say abuse comes in many forms. The worst is the abuse we heap on ourselves by not voicing our own truth.

So what can you do about it? My first piece of advice is to incorporate the "Live in the

Pink!" philosophy when you start getting to know to someone.

I'm not suggesting you use the guilty 'til proven innocent approach, but just be aware. When you start to see signs of a potentially abusive personality – leave.

For some reason, we tend to equate things like jealousy and possessiveness with intense intimacy. Now, trust me, I get it, I know that lust and sex can be heightened with these emotional rollercoasters.

It's easy to rationalize these behaviors with love because he wouldn't have started fighting that guy unless he really loved you, right? Or she wouldn't have thrown your prized auto-graphed baseball out the window unless she really wanted you to understand the depth of her love, right?

Come on. There's a healthy way to love and a not-so-healthy way. The good news is, as you exercise your power to say no and devel-op your connection with your instinct, you'll know the difference.

You'll realize that someone's inability to control her/his anger in simple situations may translate to violent behavior down the road. And while having a relationship with someone whose emotional highs are amazing might be fun, it's not worth dealing with their lows and potential abuse.

W.A.R. Tips

- Ask yourself this question: If I was walking down the street and was attacked by someone which survival technique would I want to use: fight, flight, or freeze? Hopefully through reading this book, you've aligned yourself with your inner defender and without hesitation you know you'd fight if you had to. If so, continue to have this conversation with yourself. Repetition reaps recognition. Your body will do what you mind and soul will it to do. If you're not sure which technique you want to choose, keep exploring it. Nothing's worse than indecision. There's no shame in knowing you'd rather submit and try to survive. And once you acknowledge that to yourself, you're better equipped to do it and deal with the consequences.

- If you're a victim of previous trauma (abuse, assault, accident), explore further Levine's work and others like him. There are many who have studied the effects of trapped energy in our bodies and the process of releasing that energy. You may find it very helpful.

- When you're out walking around, run through potential attack situations in your mind. Don't scare yourself, but think about what you would do if someone jumped out from behind that tree in front of you. Have an escape plan. Have a plan when you're in your house, also. Know exactly what you would do if someone came in your window or one of your doors. Knowledge is power and the more you practice this the better prepared you'll be to react.

- If you're in a relationship right now, explore the ways you show each other love. Explore the ways you show each other respect. Ask yourself if you honor yourself in your relationship, then ask if your partner honors you. These are fundamental questions in any relationship. If you can't answer them or don't like the answers you have, figure out a way to fix them. If your partner's not willing to work on it, ask yourself what you're worth.

Mass Attacks

I learned that courage was not the absence of fear, but the triumph over it. The brave man is not he who does not feel afraid, but he who conquers that fear.
Nelson Mandela

After the towers fell in New York, what could city officials offer their citizens in terms of safety tips?

After the attack at Virginia Tech, what could campus administrators tell their students?

What about during the sniper attacks in Washington D.C.?

The magnitude of these attacks is so overwhelming law enforcement finds itself reeling in an attempt to respond. But responding ineffectively isn't the worst fear safety officials suffer, what advice do they give people to prevent or survive attacks?

You can't lock down a campus. You certainly can't lock down a city. As I talk with more and more city and campus officials, the same message resonates; they have no idea what to tell their populations.

Before a tornado touches down, there are warnings. Mother Nature is not without her soft side. She gives us signs. Heck, even before lighting strikes the energy shifts and an in-tune person has a moment to get away.

But how do we help people avoid danger from something that isn't so polite?

As far as violent attacks go, the majority of them occur as one-on-one or smaller attacks. Usually the number of mass attacks that happen in the United States yearly can be counted on one hand.

However, the potential devastation from such attacks is what allows these events to invade our psyches and control our lives.

And for some reason when someone else suffers from a one-on-one attack, we manage to separate ourselves from it. We somehow justify in our minds that the situation was personal and specific to the individual involved. This may or may not be true.

Regardless, when a mass attack happens in a seemingly random way, it's harder for us to brush it aside. We start wondering what we would do in the same situation. We start wondering if it could happen to us.

I don't know why this happens. I don't know what it is about group attacks that resonate with us when single victim attacks don't. Maybe it's overexposure. Maybe we're so used to hearing about violence on a small scale that we've become immune to the implications.

Thankfully mass attacks are still rare enough they get our attention. But, the impact should be the same. The underlying vehicle of both is violence being used against people who can't or don't know how to fight back.

And in any given year, more people suffer and die from one-on-one attacks than mass attacks. But the significance of mass attacks is the terror component. It serves to hold everyone in place in the same way a pervasive fear-based culture holds women in place.

Just as the threat of danger teaches women not to walk around at night, not to be alone, not to anger a man, the terror component of mass attacks teaches people to think they're not always in control of their environment.

It teaches us to think that at any given moment our world could topple down around us and there's nothing we can do about it. That's why it works.

I use the term mass attacks to reference events such as terrorist attacks, bombings, and active shooter scenarios. I'm sure there are others, but these are the ones that come to mind based on recent events.

These situations are some of the most frustrating for government officials and law enforcement. The reason is they are impossible to predict and difficult to thwart.

Another reason is it's very tough to provide the public with hard-core training to avoid and survive them. Because of this we don't like to talk about them much. But just because there's no easy answer doesn't mean we shouldn't provide some guidance.

There are tips people can use to aid them in making decisions if they find themselves in these situations. There are tips we can provide that help people know what to look for or how to determine if someone's behavior is suspicious and should be reported.

Granted, there's no concrete, tried-and-true formula to use, but having some knowledge is better than having none.

Watch

The same three steps apply to mass attacks as they do to one-on-one attacks. Watch, assess, and react, will give you a framework for dealing with potential danger, even on a larger scale. The first step is identical.

If there's any chance to avoid an attack, it'll be apparent when you observe your surroundings. If you're living in the white zone and the fates have chosen to give you a warning sign, you won't see it or you'll see it too late to react.

Assess

As you gather information based on environments you're observing, you won't know whether you're assessing the information for a potential one-on-one attack or a mass attack.

In the initial stages, it doesn't matter. As you're going through your mental assessment just apply the same technique to everything. Does something seem out-of-the-ordinary?

If people began policing their own neighborhoods, they would know when people started hanging around who shouldn't be there. Or they would know when a house was being used as more than a typical-suburbia home.

There aren't any telltale signs to look for in preventing a mass attack. I can't tell you that every 5 foot 8 inch man with blond hair wearing a blue shirt and blue jeans walking on the south side of the street on the second Monday of every month means harm.

But that's why being constantly aware is so important. You will start to know when things aren't quite right.

As an aside, the intuitive assessment phase with larger attacks takes a slightly different angle. How many stories did you hear after the 9/11 attacks about people who were supposed to be in the towers that day and something kept them away?

How many stories do you hear about people who are supposed to be on a plane and at the last minute they change their minds only to find out later that plane crashed?

There are stories all the time about people getting an eerie feeling about something that stops them from being in the wrong place at the wrong time. Coincidence? I don't think so.

I truly believe we have our own internal survival mechanisms. The more in-tuned you are to your instinct the more apt you are to hear these messages.

Now this calls into question, did the people who died in these situations not listen to their internal messages or did they not get the messages, therefore indicating they were "meant" to die that day?

I don't know the answers to these questions. All I know is, if I'm given a message that's going to allow me to continue living a while longer, I would rather be receptive to it than not.

React

First and foremost, if a situation seems odd or feels odd, walk away. If you're at a party and you start to sense a rising level of violence, don't wait around to figure out why you feel that way. Leave.

If you're getting ready to take a trip and something doesn't feel right, don't go. Now, I'm not advocating paranoia. The art of being completely in tune with your instinct may take you a while to perfect.

Most of us have been shut off from our intuition for so long, we don't know if we're really getting a "sign" or if we're making mountains out of molehills. You may never know.

If you get a sense that something's not quite right in a situation and you leave, you may never know if something bad was about to happen. But, you do get to live to wonder.

If you find yourself in a mass attack, there are steps you can take to aid you in deciding how to react. If you are warned of an impending explosion:

- Duck and cover

- Get away from windows

- Protect your face and eyes

- Cover your nose and eyes (any little fabric will help)

If you find yourself in an active shooter scenario, your best method of response is dependent on your location and the location and intent of the shooter.

I know this is vague, but the fact remains you will be the "expert" in your situation, because you will be the only one who can decide what approach is best for you.

The very first thing you need to do is center yourself. Try not to panic. Keep telling yourself no. Find a mantra like "it's not my day to die" and keep repeating it.

Maintaining your presence of mind will aid you in the situation. At the first possible, and safe, moment, contact the authorities to report the situation. These are some of the possible reactions depending on the situation:

- Run Away

  - Don't run in a straight line (it's difficult to shoot a moving target)

  - Vary route, duck in-between buildings, find cover

- Barricade yourself

  - Silence cell phones

  - Turn off lights

  - Remain quiet

- Play dead

- Fight back

The choice to fight back is a very personal decision. No one can tell you when you should and when you shouldn't.

Some people feel that saving their own lives is the most important thing. Others will tell you saving as many other people as possible is more important. I'm not going to tell you either.

The fact remains that every situation is different and every situation requires the 3S test. Is your tactic safe, sane, and survivable?

For most people, the answer to each of these should be yes. If your plan to run away is safe, sane and survivable, then run.

If your plan to fight back is safe, sane, and survivable, then fight back.

You get the picture. However history is full of people who did things that weren't safe, sane, or survivable.

Occasionally we call those people heroes. The choice is yours. No one's going to blame you for doing what you could to survive a situation.

Unless, of course, you purposefully put another innocent person's life in peril to save your own, that's not cool.

W.A.R. Tips

- The art of redeveloping your connection with your instinct isn't easy or quick. If you're interested in spending the time and energy to reconnect, find someone who can help you. Find an energy healer or a coach or a therapist who specializes in that process. The benefits are undeniable and you'll feel more confident when assessing situations for potential danger.

- In mass attack situations, there may be a way out, even if it seems hopeless. The process of centering yourself is necessary to be able to assess the situation clearly. As you go about your day-to-day activities, start quizzing yourself. If you're walking on a campus or in a large office building, ask yourself what you would do if you heard gunfire or if the person in front of you pulled a weapon out. Start to see exit strategies as easily as you notice doors before you open them.

- Choosing to fight back: This is a viable option if you're confident you can do what it takes to beat the other person. If you're carrying a weapon, keep in mind that when law enforcement arrives, the situation will be confusing. When they get there, obey everything they say quickly. This will help identify you as someone working with them, not against them.

You're Not Alone

*Changing mass consciousness is
an individual responsibility.*
Dennis Weaver

The Myth of Separatism

One of the prevailing themes running through violent attacks, both one-on-one attacks and mass attacks, is the idea that the perpetrator felt somehow disconnected from society.

In retrospect a lot of these individuals exhibited signs of psychological separation from the rest of us.

Following the Virginia Tech incident it came out that people noticed Cho Seung-Hui showed troubling signs. One of the reasons people are able to continue seeing themselves as separate from society is we let them.

The underlying theme in the movie *Babel* addresses this phenomenon. The movie demonstrates the inherent interconnectedness of our global community.

The message of "if you want to be understood...listen" resonates in a world of individuals all searching for something. As a society we've gotten so far away from humanity we've forgotten what it looks like.

Every one of you knows someone who's suffering. You know someone who displays signs of disconnect.

When you sit in your classes, you see someone who's lonely.

When you sit in your offices, you wonder about that person who never talks to anyone and always keeps to him/herself.

What do you think happens to people who don't feel connected to society? Why do people always ask, "how could someone do that?" after a tragedy?

The kids at Columbine offer a great case study. When people don't feel like they belong to society, they start to tell themselves the rules don't apply to them.

If a person can go through his or her life day-in and day-out with feeling intimacy, caring, or consideration from anyone, what's to stop the development of thoughts outside "normal" societal standards?

I visited a college campus the other day. As I walked through the student union, I saw students sitting around talking to each other, studying, sleeping, and surfing the internet. It was great and it made me miss my undergraduate days.

As I approached the door to leave, I saw a student sitting in the corner by himself with a lost look on his face. He was staring off into space and while I couldn't put my finger on it exactly, his expression troubled me.

The best emotion I could find was emptiness. I'd never seen this guy before and probably won't ever see him again, but I walked up to him and said, "What's up? Are you doing ok?"

He looked up, surprised to be shaken out of his reverie. He stared at me for a moment with the same glazed expression.

Then I saw the haze start to disappear and his face changed. It didn't actually light up, but he looked less like someone contemplating his death or someone else's.

He said, "Yeah, I'm fine, just tired." I smiled and told him to take care. He smiled back and that was it.

It dawned on me that not so long ago I wouldn't have said anything. I would've walked by figuring that whatever was troubling this individual had nothing to do with me.

Now, don't get me wrong, I wasn't expecting a heartfelt confession that he was contemplating mass murder or didn't think he could go on with life, but it didn't matter.

The point is there was a connection. I opened myself up to the possibility that he could've just as easily looked up and told me to go to hell. But he didn't.

And the more times I do this, the more I realize people are hungry for interaction. We've cloaked ourselves in shrouds of ambivalence and apathy, but at the very heart of who we are is a need and desire to connect.

Social Consciousness

I opened this book discussing the side benefits of developing personal power. As you've gone through the chapters, hopefully you've started to realize that it's not enough for us to simply talk about personal safety.

That which keeps us safe is wrapped in self-esteem and social consciousness.

The societal factors that create dangerous situations run deeper than individuals dropping off the radar of normal behavior.

Looking at safety from a more global perspective makes it seem insurmountable. But the work starts individually. The steps are simple.

By following the W.A.R. steps you begin to realize the connection between safety and power and then you start transmitting that knowledge out to the world.

As you interact with people from a position of personal power you demonstrate this ability to others. Everything good comes from self-empowerment.

Imagine a world of self-empowered people, truly empowered, not cocky, not arrogant, not forceful, but simply powerful in their own rights.

The opportunities to commit violence severely decrease when an area's population is vigilant and impressive.

The desire to commit violence decreases when people are enjoined to participate fully in society.

The potential benefits of educating a society about power and safety aren't simply attractive, they're necessary.

So lift your heads, open your eyes, walk with confidence, observe your surroundings, trust your instinct and empower yourself to take back your personal space.

Be vigilant and Live in the Pink!

And maybe, just maybe, you'll liberate others from their fears as you liberate yourself from your own.

Q & A

Q: Do you advocate for women to venture out alone at night?

A: I advocate for women being able to do whatever they want to do without being fearful. But this is a very personal decision. It also depends on your ability to watch, assess, and react to situations.

If you don't feel supremely confident that you can handle and survive any situation you might face you need to approach every scenario with this in mind. Only operate within your own comfort zone.

But, if you desire to be able to move beyond your current comfort zone, start practicing some of the concepts I've shared with you. If you think you're weak in the intuitive assessment step, practice. If you think you're weak in your ability to physically react, practice. Find mentors, coaches, or guides who can help you.

There are spiritual teachers who can help put you in touch with your inner knowing and there are trainers who can help develop your physical strength and accuracy.

Just remember - there are no rules about what people (men or women) can or can't do. You're only limited by your own fear and willingness to step outside of it.

Q: I was abused by my boyfriend in college, how can I get over that experience and empower myself?

A: The short answer is - do what I've said in this book and develop the confidence to approach situations from an empowered position.

By giving yourself the tools to approach the situation differently were it to happen again, you make strides in getting through the debilitating effects of the previous experience.

The longer answer is - my take on past traumas is a little different from most. I don't think you can release yourself from an event by rehashing it over and over. There are experts who think past traumas continue to plague people because of what we did with our energy during the event.

Peter Levine, in *Waking the Tiger*, talks about our animal nature and the role it plays in moving beyond traumatic experiences. Most people are familiar with the flight or fight concept. Well, there is a third option that is more prevalent and more detrimental than the other two. This is the freezing or playing dead option.

Levine explores what happens with energy in our bodies when playing dead and the future effects of this process if we don't fully understand it. Without getting into his entire thesis, I will say that the way to get over a traumatic experience is to get through it.

It's not enough to "deal with it" and move on. Most of us approach life in this way without realizing the horrifying effects it has on our bodies and our ability to live freely.

For this reason, I'm so passionate about people approaching perilous situations from a position of power. Not only will it increase your chances of survival, but it will increase your chances of moving through the experience without traumatizing your body and causing debilitating fears for years after.

Q: At what age should I start teaching my children about power and safety?

A: Ultimately those are two different questions. The concept of personal power encompasses everything we are. As we teach our children who they are, how we perceive them, how they perceive themselves, we give them inherent messages about power. This starts *in utero.*

As parents we deliver messages to our children mentally, physically and spiritually. Our feelings and thoughts about ourselves and our own personal power translate freely and easily to our children. From that perspective, you have no choice in the matter. You start teaching your children about power from the moment they exist in your world.

Regarding teaching your children about safety, this is a very personal decision. On some level, you're always teaching your children about safety. "Don't touch the stove, it's hot." "Don't put a fork in the electrical outlet, it won't go well." As parents we often repeat the same phrases we heard as children, sometimes despite our best attempts to the contrary.

I can share how my husband and I approach concepts of safety with our youngest daughter. We try to allow her to learn for herself. Obviously there are constraints like it's best not to let your children learn the fork in the outlet example firsthand, but we have a lot of leeway in other areas.

When she was a year old she was fascinated with the fireplace. I let her sit on my lap and help me put logs in the fire. I talked to her about the process and explained that this was strictly a mommy-baby or daddy-baby activity. We're very fortunate because our daughter is contemplative and fairly wise for her age. She has a healthy respect for things that might hurt her, but allows her curiosity to push her to discover.

We set the standard rules like, "We always hold hands in a parking lot," and she enjoys invoking this rule on her own. She stops at the end of sidewalks and proudly announces the impending "parky ot" while holding out her hand.

We spend a lot of time explaining things to her and demonstrating consequences. She has a rocking horse she loves and discovered if she leans back while rocking really hard, the front ends of the rockers leave the floor. We explained to her the likelihood of the horse flipping backwards.

I offered to demonstrate for her what might happen if she continued riding that way. She agreed. So I told her to start riding and then flipped her backwards. She hit the floor in a controlled way, but with enough of a jolt she decided her new game wasn't so fun.

It takes a lot more time than simply telling her not to do something, but the power she feels knowing she made that decision on her own is priceless. She's two.

Bonus Articles

From the Hen House to the Lion Den
By Tonya Dawn   09/17/07

On Thursday four women were sexually assaulted at the University of Maryland, three of them were in the same house, a sorority house, and one of those three was raped.

My first question isn't how did this happen? It's how did this man think it was safe to walk into a house full of women?

How? Because we've taught him it's safe.

As a society, as women, we've taught him he has nothing to fear by walking into a home containing at least three women and taking whatever he wants. I don't know all the details of the attacks, I'm simply piecing them together from media reports. But the fact remains, three women were assaulted, one was raped, and this man isn't dead, maimed, or injured in any way.

That fact alone is enough to make me sick. But, to add fuel to the fire, I was on the phone all morning calling staff and officials at the University of Maryland. I spoke to one woman who's a victims' advocate for the university.

As I told her about my mission in the world, to empower people to avoid these situations and react powerfully if one occurs, she informed me that while they have no problem empowering women, of course, they didn't really want to send the message that this could have been prevented.

I was floored.

I recovered and let her know that I understand it's anti-productive to tell victims they could've prevented an attack, but there's a huge difference between blaming the victim and empowering people overall to take back their personal space. Her reaction says it all.

As women, as a society, we've tried to treat sexual assaults and violent attacks as something that's wrong with the perpetrators. No doubt, something's wrong with people who use violence as a means of expression.

But I for one am not willing to sit around and wait for their rehabilitation or therapy sessions to kick in. The fact that our first reaction isn't outrage tells me where we stand as a society.

Another example, a few weeks ago I was scouting out self-defense and personal safety classes in Dallas and was told to my face, by a man, that if a man wants to physically take something from a woman, he's going to win every time.

This is what men believe. And worse yet, this is what women believe.

How did we get here? How did a sorority house full of women become a hen house instead of a lion den? How did we become a society of women who freeze and cower in the face of opposition instead of becoming enraged and calling on our internal power to save us?

Have you ever seen a woman in rage? What happened to hell hath no fury? We can become outraged when someone cheats on us, tear up the seats of his car, burn down his house, but when someone steps into our personal space we forget our natural state as survivors.

As a society, our response has been to pat victims on their backs, offer them support groups, and secretly pray it doesn't happen to us.

Well, it has happened to us. It's happened to each of us because every time we allow something like this to pass without understanding the impact it has on us as a whole, we reenact the powerlessness all over again.

Every time we have a group of young women who don't know they have the right and the strength to fight back we lose. I'm tired of hearing that there's nothing we can do about it. This sit and wait and hope the next "1-in-3" isn't you is ridiculous.

I for one say bring it on. Let a man try to walk into a house I live in and take anything from me while I'm there. I might not kill him, but guaranteed he's gonna be hurting.

Until we adopt this attitude that we are dangerous, no one else is going to believe us. Until we take back our homes, our apartments, our sorority houses, our neighborhoods, our schools, our bodies, no one's going to do it for us.

Think about it, how tempted would a man be to walk into a sorority house if the last man who did it got his ass beat?

Make no mistake about it - I'm not blaming the victims here. No one has the right to blame women who have been victimized in the past.

I've been victimized in the past. And the sad thing is, I don't need anyone to ask me what I could've done differently in the situation to prevent it. I asked myself that question for years. I don't know a single victim who doesn't ask herself that question.

So by us keeping our mouths shut and not bringing that conversation to the forefront, we're not doing anyone any favors. Trust me, you can't heap any more distress on a victim of sexual assault than she heaps on herself. So why not do something productive?

By all means, let's acknowledge that total and complete blame lies on perpetrators of these crimes, but so what? I've got news for you, the people, typically men, who commit these crimes aren't cringing with fear because we think they're bad people. But let them get the crap beat out of them once or twice and they might rethink their hobbies.

It's not possible, right? It's not possible for women to overpower men, right? Of course it is.

We've come so far away from our inner warriors, we've forgotten who they are. If I was a conspiracy theorist, I would be able to provide all kinds of reasons why women are convinced they're powerless. I'd be able to point to a patriarchal system and years of oppression.

But, again, who cares? That does us no good right now. What does help us is acknowledging that we've been doing ourselves a disservice by cuddling and coddling our fear and making ourselves feel okay about being scared.

By all means, be afraid, not that you might get attacked, raped, or killed, be afraid that you've given up years of your life to the belief that you're somehow "less than" or weak.

And then get over it.

We have a point to make and some hobbies to change. Because until we stop squawking about the big bad fox invading the hen house and start lamenting the fate of the poor fox that was stupid enough to step into the lion den, we only have ourselves to blame.

Truly, call it what you want, but we're the only ones who can change this. And we're powerful enough to do it.

Conflict Resolution or Heart-Centered Communication

By Tonya Dawn   12/18/11

For some reason as 2011 snuggles into its cocoon, preparing to emerge as bright and shiny 2012, the concept of conflict resolution seems to be foremost on people's minds. The number of requests I receive to demystify the process of resolving conflict in an intrinsically powerful way is a bit confounding. It seems counterintuitive that conflict runs through minds as "Have a Holly, Jolly Christmas" plays in the background.

But for whatever reason, it's there. And the question never becomes, "How do I avoid conflict?" I think as a society we feel that attempting to avoid conflict is passive and weak, that somehow conflict is inevitable and a necessary part of growth for an organization or relationship.

Maybe it is, but not as we typically define it. When people ask me about conflict resolution, they really just want me to show them some cool techniques for winning an argument...every time. They fall in love with the sexy aspect of counterintelligence, the part they equate to our ability to wave our hand in front of someone's face and say, "These are not the droids you are looking for." (I couldn't resist.)

So when I look them in the face and ask, "During this conflict, did you speak from your mind or from your heart?" I get a wide-eyed, confused expression, with a lace of what's-this-crazy-hippy-talking-about thrown in. And therein lies the problem. Conflict only happens between egos. It's about harsh words, staunch stances and the battle between right and wrong. Our spirits do not engage in conflict. Our hearts do not engage in conflict. It's just not possible.

Unfortunately, we created a situation in our society where confidence and power too often balance precariously on our egos. The issue, of course, is no one wins when egos get involved. When a conversation turns to a battle of wills and thought processes, it ceases to become merely an event of shared ideas and turns into something ugly and counterproductive.

So what's the answer? Ironically, it's actually the easiest thing in the world to do, but the most difficult to swallow...initially. (Trust me, it gets easier with practice.) The absolute best way to resolve conflict is to avoid it. I know, I know, profundity at its finest, but hear me out. The same method for avoiding conflict can be used even in the midst of conflict to resolve it. But you're going to have to trust me on this one...

Simply speak from your heart.

It can't be that easy, can it? Surely I'm not suggesting that touchy-feely tactics have any place in business (or relationships for that matter).

It can and I am. But the process of getting there confounds. In a world that promotes people based on their ability to shed blood and proceed without emotion, the idea of heart-centered communication typically resides in spiritual discussions and liberal arts programs.

And that's unfortunate.

Whether you're sitting in a board room as tensions heat up or at your desk holding the telephone receiver five inches from your ear as the yelling ensues, the only surefire tactic to squash conflict is to resist the urge to match ego with ego. One person in the conversation must choose to take the high road. Not from a pedestal perspective, but from a true desire to achieve results rather than argue viewpoint.

Does this translate into showing weakness? Because that's really the fear, isn't it? If we don't bloviate as well as the next person how can we be taken seriously? If someone attacks us with verbal wits and sharp-tongueedness, doesn't protocol demand we retaliate in kind? Absolutely. But that doesn't make it right or progressive.

Picture this: You're sitting in a board room as Joan and Betty start a "discussion" about their vision for the company's marketing efforts in 2012. Joan believes in every ounce of her being that the company must market more heavily to women because the growing number of female entrepreneurs is an untapped market in your industry. Betty looks at the charts for 2011 and points to the tried-

and-true methods used as the only safe option.

The discussion quickly turns ugly because they refuse to acknowledge that both viewpoints address the question at hand. Both are viable options and both have the same potential to produce results. But because egos quickly translate a debate like this into self-worth, the communication becomes less about finding a solution and more about one-up*person*ship.

All witnesses to this event start to sense the tension and no one quite knows what to do. A truly skilled manager may step into the situation and acknowledge both points of view and encourage a discussion amongst the group of pros and cons to each side. This takes the heat off a bit and shifts focus from Joan and Betty. But the underlying tension between those two still remains.

And for what? At any point in time either Joan or Betty easily could have taken a deep breath, forced the energy from her head to her heart, and started by giving credit to the other point of view. Once this happens the other person is likely to respond in kind. On the rare occasion that the second person is so wrapped up in her argument she fails to see she's only arguing with herself, it may take some careful and conscious communication to talk her down, but anyone with a modicum of self-awareness quickly sees the futility in her approach at that point.

Now the two can discuss the issue without emotion and may discover a collaborative option, one that benefits from both perspectives.

I struggle with using Joan and Betty for this scenario because the process is just as likely to occur between two men or between a man and a woman. I don't mean to suggest this only happens between women (the eternal writers' pronoun plague won out over gender heterogeneity).

It's a simple example, but that's how quickly these situations explode. And the process of shifting energy from your head to heart is the fastest want to avoid or diffuse any conflict. I'm not suggesting opinions won't differ or that everyone has to hold hands and sing Kum Ba Yah, but heart-centered discussions have a much better chance of resulting in progressive, collaborative, and innovative ideas than do ego-centered or mind-centered battles.

Try it. If you're not completely satisfied, go back to talking from your head. But I contend that over time you'll experience skyrocketed success in any communication situation by employing this simple technique. Even Luke Skywalker had to learn to remove his ego from a situation in order to harness the force. (Yeah, yeah, I'll stop...)

About the Author

Tonya Dawn Recla's heart and soul lie in two things: her family and her passion to change the world. She initiates this change by teaching women about personal POWER based on what she learned chasing spies.

Her experience as an Army soldier and U.S. Government Special Agent combined with graduate education as a social scientist led her to discover the elusive connection between personal POWER and safety.

Tonya's Live in the Pink!™ concept encourages women to live in awareness and harness the POWER in every moment.

A gifted speaker, Tonya is available for keynotes, workshops, seminars and one-on-one training.

You can learn more about her at PersonalPOWERexperts.com.

Made in the USA
Columbia, SC
08 July 2021